A ROOKIE READER

OUT THE DOOR

By Catherine Matthias
Illustrations by Eileen Mueller Neill

Prepared under the direction of Robert Hillerich, Ph.D.

CHILDRENS PRESS ™

CHICAGO

Library of Congress Cataloging in Publication Data

Matthias, Catherine.
  Out the door.

  (A Rookie reader)
  Summary: Simple text and illustrations follow
a child's progress from home to school and back
again.
  I. Neill, Eileen Mueller, ill. II. Title.
III. Series.
PZ7.M43470u   [E]   81-17060
ISBN 0-516-03560-6   AACR2

Out the door.

In the door.

Out the door. Down the steps.

Up the steps.

Down the steps. Down the sidewalk.

Around…and around…

and around the puddle.

Into the puddle.

Down the sidewalk.

At the bus stop.

Onto the bus.

Off the bus.

Onto the bus.

At the school.

Into the school.

Off with the hat.

Off with the coat.

Off with the boots.

Into the room.

Down at the desk.

Work . . . and play.

Work...and play.

On with the hat.

On with the coat.

On with the boots.

Out of the school.

Onto the bus.

Off the bus.

Onto the bus.

Riding…and riding…and riding.

At the bus stop.

Off the bus.

Onto the bus.

Off the bus.

Down the sidewalk.

Off with the hat. Off with the coat.

Into the puddle.

Up the steps.

Down the steps.

Up the steps.

In the door.

Out the door.

In the door.

Word List

	hat	riding
and	in	room
around	into	school
at	of	sidewalk
boots	off	steps
bus	on	stop
coat	onto	the
desk	out	up
door	play	with
down	puddle	work

About the Author

Catherine Matthias grew up in a small town in southern New Jersey. As a child, she loved swimming, bicycling, snow, and small animals. *Wind in the Willows* and *The Little House* were her favorite books.

She started writing her own children's stories while teaching pre-school in Philadelphia. *Too Many Balloons* and *Out the Door* are her first published books.

Catherine now lives with her family in the Northwest, where her favorite things are gardening, hiking, fog, windy autumn days, and the ocean.

About the Artist

Eileen Mueller Neill, a native of the Midwest, received her art training at The Columbus College of Art and Design, Columbus, Ohio. After graduation, she held a design illustrator position with a Detroit art studio. She presently works with her husband Jim, a graphic designer, and over the past several years, she has done illustrations for a number of children's books.

Eileen, Jim, and their children, Kim, Kelly, and Kia, live in Riverwoods, Illinois, where they spend their leisure hours flying 'Fantasia,' their hot air balloon.